White Key Majors and Minors

Splattered with Fun!

A Collection of

Later Elementary Level Piano Solos

by

Glenda Austin

Glenda Austin

A native of Missouri, Glenda received a Bachelors degree in music education and a Masters in piano performance from the University of Missouri. A member of several academic and artistic honorary organizations, Ms. Austin has been commissioned by several piano and music organizations to compose piano pieces including *Clavier* magazine. Glenda's pieces are popular with both students and teachers of all ages. As past president of the Joplin Piano Teachers Association, she remains musically active in teaching, community theater, church choirs, adjudicating piano festivals and has served as a clinician for piano pedagogy workshops on the local, state and national levels. Many of her pieces have been placed on the National Federation of Music Clubs and Junior Festival lists. Married with two children, Glenda resides in Joplin, Missouri.

From the Composer

In the following collection of white key majors and minors, the pieces are designed to sound more difficult than they really are. This is an excellent way to make your students feel successful playing in different key signatures. The pieces may be taught individually or in groups of two's (parallel majors and minors). The marked fingering should be followed closely; however, one should never hesitate to add personal touches! Enjoy the variety of selections and remember to try and match your music to the titles!

White Key Majors and Minors

Splattered with Fun!

A Collection of Later Elementary Level Piano Solos

by

Glenda Austin

CONTENTS

12158

Back Talk
(C Major)

Animated

Glenda Austin

Thunderstorm
(C Minor)

Aggressively throughout

Glenda Austin

Gliding High

(D Major)

Glenda Austin

Procession
(D Minor)

Glenda Austin

The Whiskery Walrus
(E Major)

Glenda Austin

Relaxed and flowing

f
f
rit.
D.C. al Coda
Coda
rit.
8vb

Shadow Tag
(E Minor)

Quickly

Glenda Austin

p
mf
f
mp
mf
p

Tag Team
(F Major)

Precisely

Glenda Austin

Midnight Chase

(F Minor)

Glenda Austin

Smooth Sailing
(G Major)

Glenda Austin

Mysterious Visitor
(G Minor)

Glenda Austin

A Sunny Day

(A Major)

Carefree

Glenda Austin

Autumn Morning

(A Minor)

Glenda Austin

Smoothly and not too fast

A Sunday Stroll
(B Major)

Stately

Glenda Austin

Rolling Clouds

(B Minor)

Evenly

Glenda Austin

L.H.
mp
4
5
mf
rit.
R.H.
a tempo
f
L.H.
L.H.
no ritard.
f
R.H.